Heaven:

A Journal of Thoughts
and Reflections

by
JONI EARECKSON TADA

Heaven: A Journal of Thoughts and Reflections

ISBN 0-310-96554-3

Excerpts taken from *Heaven, Our Real Home*

Copyright © 1995 by Joni Eareckson Tada

Requests for information should be addressed to:
  Zondervan Publishing House
  5300 Patterson Avenue, SE
  Grand Rapids, MI 49530

Project Editor: Sarah Hupp
Editorial Assistant: Steve Jensen
Design: Robin O'Brien

Printed in the United States of America

97 96 95 /❖ RRD-C / 3 2 1

Table of Contents

To:_____

May the following pages
help you tune into heaven's melody
and show you the way home.

From:_____

W hether we are adults or children, our best memories are usually the sort that, like a tuning fork, strike a resonant chord in our souls. It's a song we never quite forget and recognize immediately whenever we catch its echo. We recognize it because it is so full of heartbreaking beauty. Like deep calling to deep, it is stamped with God's imprint; and since we bear his image, the memory is sealed in that deepest, most profound part of us. Such moments cast soundings and plumb the real depths of who we are. And what we hear is a heavenly echo.

The first time I heard that haunting, heavenly song was in the summer of 1957. We were heading west through the country roads of Kansas. Daddy had pulled the car over onto the gravel shoulder. I jumped out of the sweltering back seat ... picked up a piece of gravel ... then heaved the stone ... far out into the biggest, widest, longest field I had ever seen. It was an ocean of wheat, waves of golden grain rippling in the wind. Except for the hissing sound of summertime bugs, all was quiet, incredibly quiet.

Or was it?

I can't remember if the song came from the sky or the field, or if it were just the sound of crickets. I tried hard to listen, but instead of actually hearing notes, I felt ... space. A wide-open space filling my heart, as if the entire wheat field could fit into my seven-year-old soul. I had never felt—or was it heard—such a thing. Yet, as soon as I tried to grasp the haunting echo, it vanished.

I was only seven, but standing there by the barbed wire fence of a Kansas wheat field, I knew my heart had been broken by God. I kept staring while humming an old Sunday school favorite, *This world is not my home, I'm just a passin' through.* For me, the moment was heavenly.

Rather than let that song retire in the presence of mundane things like scratchy AM radios and grinding dishwashers ... I love to think and read about heaven. Actual mountains and clouds are exalting, but even the most beautiful displays of earth's glory—

towering thunderheads above a wheat field or the view of the Grand Canyon from the south rim—are only rough sketches of heaven. Earth's best is only a dim reflection, a preliminary rendering of the glory that will one day be revealed. This is why the heavenly song is still an echo. It's a yearning, unfulfilled. A longing that is still an ache.

Heaven will not be an *unmaking* of all the good things we know, but a new-and-vastly-improved version. Heaven will also be an *undoing* of all the bad things we know as God wipes away every tear and closes the curtain on pain and disappointment. I look forward to heaven because I have a lot invested there. A new body. A new heart free of sin.

Heaven has been, and always shall be, a matter of faith. If heaven is the home of your spirit, the rest for your soul, the repository of every spiritual investment on earth, then it must grip your heart. And your heart must grip heaven by faith.

Step back for a moment, focus your eyes of faith and then walk with me into a world you've heard about from your youth but have never seen: Heaven ... your journey's end, your life's goal, your purpose for going on. Look with me through a glass darkly and you just might discover that Home is closer—and more real—than you ever thought.

For Reflection

What makes you long *eagerly* for heaven? If you have ever had the sense that heaven is your real home, what was that sensation like? Where were you and what were you doing? If you haven't sensed that resonant chord yet, what could you do to tune your ears of faith to hear that song?

_____

_____

_____

_____

_____

But our citizenship is in heaven. And we eagerly await a Savior from there, the Lord Jesus Christ.
Philippians 3:20

What's So Great About Heaven

I Belong There

This life is not forever. We believers *are* headed for heaven. It is reality. Heaven may be as near as next year, or next week, so it makes good sense to spend some time here on earth thinking candid thoughts about that marvelous future reserved for us.

For Reflection

What are your candid thoughts about heaven? Make a short list of things about heaven on which you want to meditate so that your mind is "set on things above." Is there anything about heaven about which you are afraid or unsure?

_____

_____

_____

_____

_____

_____

_____

_____

_____

_____

_____

_____

Set your minds on things above, not on earthly things.
Colossians 3:2

Heaven's Symbolism

Heaven is often described in terms of "no this" and "no that." No more night. No more moon. The positive descriptions about what heaven *is* seem clumsy and ungraceful. Streets of gold ... pearly gates. Heaven can't be reduced to terms we can manage. Simply put, there are no words for heaven.

For Reflection

When you read the words that describe heaven at face value—gates of pearl, streets of gold—what impression is created in your mind? If the images are viewed as clues in an amazing mystery, now how do you respond? What are the clues telling you about the positives of heaven?

Then I saw a new heaven
and a new earth, for the first
heaven and the first earth
had passed away, and there
was no longer any sea.
Revelation 21:1

What's So Great About Heaven

Through Eyes of Faith

When you take time to ponder Scripture, your faith has something to hold onto ... something that's factual and true ... something from which your dreams about heaven can take root. When it comes to heaven, there's no limit to what the Lord will confide to those whose faith is rooted in Scripture.

For Reflection

What are the things about heaven in which you have absolute confidence? Record your praise to God for such confidences because he has put them in your heart. What are the things about heaven about which you are still unsure? Pray for the courage to believe.

So keep up your courage, men, for I have faith in God that it will happen just as he told me. Acts 27:25

What's So Great About Heaven

See Heaven's Positive Side

When it comes to heaven ... *the negatives are used in order to show us the positive.* On earth, we know all too well what the negatives are. Suffering, pain and death. Show us their opposites, the positive side, and we shall have the best possible idea of the perfect state.

For Reflection

Scripture encourages us with its list of negatives about heaven. No more sorrow. No more crying. No more pain. No more death. What negatives encourage you the most? Why? How will your sufferings be used to glorify God?

On no day will its gates ever be shut, for there will be no night there. Revelation 21:25

What's So Great About Heaven

New Bodies

One day the dream will come true. One day no more bulging middles and balding tops. No varicose veins or crow's feet. Forget the thunder thighs and highway hips. Just a quick leapfrog over the tombstone and it's the body you've always dreamed of. Fit and trim, smooth and sleek.

For Reflection

Reflect on Christ's resurrection body and record its characteristics. How do you respond to that picture when you understand that your body will be like his? How will you spend eternity with this new body?

_____

_____

_____

_____

_____

_____

_____

_____

_____

_____

_____

_____

_____

But our citizenship is in heaven. And we eagerly await a Savior from there, the Lord Jesus Christ, who, by the power that enables him to bring everything under his control, will transform our lowly bodies so that they will be like his glorious body.
Philippians 3:20-21

How Are the Dead Raised?

No one knows ... how life can spring from a dead seed. Not even a Ph.D. in Botany. It's one of God's miracles of nature. So it will be with the resurrection. It is no more difficult to believe in the resurrection than it is to believe in the harvest.

For Reflection

Is there anything about death which frightens you? How does the assurance of resurrection dispel that fear? Make a list of loved ones who have died and reflect on the joy they will experience on resurrection day. Reflect on your joy in reuniting with them.

But someone may ask,
"How are the dead raised?
With what kind of body will
they come?" How foolish!
What you sow does not
come to life unless it dies.
1 Corinthians 15:35-36

What Kind of Body?

Somehow, somewhere within that acorn is the promise and pattern of the tree it will become. Somehow, somewhere within you is the pattern of the heavenly person you will become. You—and one day what you will be—are one and the same, yet different.

For Reflection

What do you see in you that serves as a pattern of the heavenly person you will become? As you answer this question, include those characteristics God has developed in you that reflect the image of his Son.

_____

_____

_____

_____

_____

_____

_____

_____

_____

_____

_____

_____

_____

When you sow, you do not plant the body that will be, but just a seed, perhaps of wheat or of something else. But God gives it a body as he has determined, and to each kind of seed he gives its own body.

1 Corinthians 15:37-38

A Perfect Body and Soul

To appreciate the perfection of our bodies and souls, we have to begin to get our hearts and minds somewhat in tune for heaven. Heaven is a prepared place for prepared people. Otherwise heaven is a turn-off.

For Reflection

What are you doing to prepare for heaven? What characteristics of your spirit do you want God to develop so that you are made perfect on the day of Christ Jesus? Commit those characteristics to God, petitioning him to do the work in you, regardless of the cost.

Be perfect, therefore, as your
heavenly Father is perfect.
Matthew 5:48

What's So Great About Heaven

Perfect People in Perfect Fellowship

Heaven's wedding supper of the Lamb will be the perfect party. The Father has been sending out invitations and people have been RSVP'ing through the ages. And like any party, what will make it sweet is the fellowship. Fellowship with our glorious Savior and with our friends and family.

For Reflection

Who are you waiting to see in heaven? Family? Friends? Visualize one particular person and consider how your relationship with that person will change in heaven. Reflect on your time with Jesus in heaven. How will your relationship with him differ from what you experience now?

_____

_____

_____

_____

_____

_____

_____

_____

_____

_____

_____

_____

Then the angel said to me,
"Write: 'Blessed are those
who are invited to the wedding supper of the Lamb!'"
And he added, "These are
the true words of God."
Revelation 19:9

What's So Great About Heaven

To Bow in Worship

The first thing I plan to do on resurrected legs is to drop on grateful, glorified knees. To *not* move will be my chance to demonstrate heartfelt thanks to the Lord. To not move will be my last chance to present a sacrifice of praise—paralyzed praise.

For Reflection

How will you express your gratitude and praise to Jesus when you are in heaven? What heavenly privilege would you sacrifice in order to glorify and praise God?

_____

_____

_____

_____

_____

_____

_____

_____

_____

_____

_____

_____

_____

_____

In a loud voice they sang: "Worthy is the Lamb, who was slain, to receive power and wealth and wisdom and strength and honor and glory and praise!"
Revelation 5:12

Faith to Find Your Way Home

What it takes to know the place Jesus has gone ahead to prepare is faith. Faith in what God has to say about heaven from his Word. Faith that focuses not *on* the scriptural symbols, but *inside* and *beyond* them. Faith that shows you the way home.

For Reflection

Focus your eyes of faith. Bring heaven forward into vivid reality in your thoughts. Involve your heart and your eyes. What do you see of heaven? Of Jesus? What one promise of Scripture helps your faith in the reality of heaven the most?

_____

_____

_____

_____

_____

_____

_____

_____

_____

_____

_____

_____

_____

_____

I pray also that the eyes of
your heart may be enlightened
in order that you may know
the hope to which he has
called you, the riches of his
glorious inheritance in the
saints. *Ephesians 1:18*

*A*s a child I wondered where God lived in outer space and how long it would take to get there. Had I been old enough to read an astronomy textbook, I would have discovered a few statistics that would have blown me out of the water. Our solar system has a diameter of about 700 light-minutes. That's 8 billion miles. But the galaxy in which our solar system is contained has a diameter of 100,000 light-years. Not minutes, but *years*. Our galaxy is immense. Yet our little galaxy that is 100,000 light-years wide is just *one* of billions of other galaxies out in the cosmos. Billions of stars and planets, all created by God.

What *is* on the other side?

The *Scientific Journal* may be stymied by that question, but not the Bible. Far beyond intergalactic space with its billions of swirling nebulae and novas lies another dimension. You could call it infinity, but wherever it is and however far out, the Bible calls it the highest of the heavens ... the abode of God (Deuteronomy 10:14).

Yet even though the dwelling place of God may be a long way up, distances like "up" and "down" lose their meaning when you realize that heaven—even the highest heavens—exists beyond our space-time continuum. Latitude and longitude, as well as directions and distances are related to time, and time is a part of the fourth dimension ... only a small part of infinity. Time there will be swallowed up.

You cannot get *transported* to heaven. You cannot get there in a rocket ship. That's because heaven exists beyond even speeded-up time. The kingdom of heaven over which Jesus is, and was and ever shall be King, is a place, but more so, a dimension where time and distances are not obstacles.

Faith assures us that heaven is *transcendent*. It is beyond the limits of our experience; it exists apart from our material universe. Heaven is also *immanent* in that it envelops all the celestial bodies, swirling galaxies and the starry hosts. Heaven is closer than we imagine even though we can't see it.

I get tickled thinking about how rock-solid … how like the Rock of Gibraltar heaven is. In the midst of it all, the glittering capital city of heaven, the New Jerusalem, will be set like a gleaming pearl. Kings and princes will pour into the Holy City from the far corners of the earth to pay homage. The image blows my mind, but it's laid out as clear as crystal glass in Revelation 21.

I have an idea that when we step into infinity, I won't be the only one who, with new resurrected legs, will drop on grateful glorified knees. Tens of thousands will have the same idea. We will feel utterly at home in the golden throne room of the King. We'll gape in wide-eyed wonder at so much light, praise and glory!

In heaven, there will be no failure in service. We will serve God through worship and work—exciting work of which we never grow tired. No disappointment in doing. We will never struggle with failing to do the task God puts before us. We will never fall short of meeting our responsibilities. We will sit with Christ on His throne and reign with Him.

We shall touch and taste, rule and reign, move and run, laugh and never have reason to cry. Heaven will feel like home. I will be a co-heir with Christ … I will help rule in the new heavens and the new earth … and I will be busier and happier in service than I ever dreamed possible. And you will be, too.

For Reflection

Think about your endless day in heaven. What will you do as you worship? What kind of service do you think you will engage in for God? What will you learn and explore?

_____

_____

_____

_____

_____

_____

But in keeping with his promise we are looking forward to a new heaven and a new earth, the home of righteousness. 2 Peter 3:13

Heaven Is Real

Heaven is not some Never-Never-Land of thin, ghostly shapes and clouds. It's not a place where you can poke your finger through people only to discover that they are spacey spirit-beings you can't really hug or hold. No way! Heaven is concrete ... rock-solid real ... a home—much more so than earth.

For Reflection

Have you ever thought that heaven was a wispy, nebulous place? Did you know that earth is the place of withering grass and heaven is rock-solid? How could heaven be "more real" or "more rock-solid?" What makes earth like grass—elusive, temporary, unreal?

Heaven is my throne, and the earth is my footstool. What kind of house will you build for me? says the Lord. Or where will my resting place be? Acts 7:49

Where Is Heaven and What Is It Like?

Rewards in Heaven

God wants to award me a crown! The child in me jumps up and down to think God might actually award me something. Nothing is so obvious in a heavenly-minded child of God as his undisguised pleasure in receiving a reward—a reward that reflects the approval of the Father.

For Reflection

You are the fulfillment of God's desire. In fact, you give him so much pleasure, he has a gift for you, a reward—a crown. What will your reward be? And for what will you be rewarded?

Now there is in store for me
the crown of righteousness,
which the Lord, the righteous
Judge, will award to me on
that day—and not only to me,
but also to all who have
longed for his appearing.
2 Timothy 4:8

The Judgment Seat of Christ

We will bring to the judgment seat of Christ all that we are and all that we've done. One look from the Lord will scrutinize the quality of what we've built and selfish service will be consumed in a fiery flash. Some will walk away scalded from the heat; their only reward will be their eternal salvation.

For Reflection

As you look forward to the judgment seat of Christ, what areas or actions in your life do you see as being consumed in the fire? What godly motives exist in your heart that you are confident Christ will reward? What motives do you need to confess that are displeasing to him?

_____

_____

_____

_____

_____

_____

_____

_____

_____

_____

_____

_____

Therefore judge nothing before the appointed time; wait till the Lord comes. He will bring to light what is hidden in darkness and will expose the motives of men's hearts. At that time each will receive his praise from God.
1 Corinthians 4:5

Eternal, Loving Worship

In heaven, praise won't be inert and abstract ... a musty, old hymn sung by a handful of stone-faced worshipers in a huge cathedral. Praise in heaven will have substance. We will no longer desire our God who is absent, but rejoice in our God who is present.

For Reflection

Think about the most meaningful worship experience you've ever had. What made it so meaningful? Reflect on how much more meaningful your worship will be in heaven. How will God's visible presence affect your worship? What can you do to cultivate worship on earth as a prelude to your worship in heaven?

Sing to him, sing praise to him; tell of all his wonderful acts. Glory in his holy name; let the hearts of those who seek the LORD rejoice.
Psalm 105:2-3

Serving God in Heaven

When it comes to blessing us ... God is already thinking exponentially, as in his "ten cities" equation. He generously raises your capacity for service. The more faithful you are in this life, the more responsibility you will be given in the life to come.

For Reflection

Do you love serving God? How have you been faithful in service for him here on earth? Faithful to a struggling marriage? Sharing the gospel with a neighbor? What "small" thing is God bringing to mind this week in which you can be faithful?

_____

_____

_____

_____

_____

_____

_____

_____

_____

_____

_____

_____

_____

"Well done, my good servant!" his master replied. "Because you have been trustworthy in a very small matter, take charge of ten cities." Luke 19:17

Where Is Heaven and What Is It Like?

Ruling Over Earth

Time and again, the words "inheritance," "earth," and "reign" appear together in Scripture. The particulars may not be laid out, but there's one hint we're supposed to get: We will reign with Christ over the earth.

For Reflection

How does the fact of our future reign affect your thinking about being a Christian? Why would Christ share his inheritance and his reign with us?

Blessed and holy are those who have part in the first resurrection. The second death has no power over them, but they will be priests of God and of Christ and will reign with him for a thousand years. Revelation 20:6

The Edge of the Universe

With the snap of a finger and a few images from the Hubble space telescope, astronomers are agreeing that the universe had a beginning. They also agree the universe will have an ending. I wonder if scientists have thought to pick up the book of Revelation for a sneak preview.

For Reflection

Thank the Lord for the creation you see. Then thank the Lord for the creation you cannot see—the new earth, the new heaven, the endless day. Reflect on how much more wonderful the new creation will be than the one we have now.

_____

_____

_____

_____

_____

_____

_____

_____

_____

_____

_____

_____

_____

_____

*In the beginning God created
the heavens and the earth.*
Genesis 1:1

Where Is Heaven and What Is It Like?

The Time of the End

I wish the prophet Daniel could have lived to see this day. Then again, maybe he did. Perhaps he saw CNN in some prophetic vision and could only watch in wide-eyed wonder ... and he turned away just in time to hear God say, "Close up ... the words of the scroll. ... "

For Reflection

Think about what we now know about our world and its inhabitants. How much more do you think there is to learn? Have we entered that era described to Daniel as "the time of the end" when many would go about gaining knowledge?

_____

_____

_____

_____

_____

_____

_____

_____

_____

_____

_____

_____

But you, Daniel, close up and seal the words of the scroll until the time of the end. Many will go here and there to increase knowledge.
Daniel 12:4

Where Is Heaven and What Is It Like?

How Close Is Heaven?

Heaven is close. Perhaps closer than we imagine. It's a little like ...
an unborn infant in his mother's womb. There he is, safe in his little
world, ignorant of the fact that a more glorious world is enclosing
and encasing his.

For Reflection

How can heaven be closer than we imagine yet beyond our universe? What impact does your nearness to heaven have on you? If
we are nearer to heaven than our eyes can see, what does that say
about the closeness of God and the hosts of heaven? What impact
does God's nearness to us have on you?

_____

_____

_____

_____

_____

_____

_____

_____

_____

_____

_____

_____

Jesus answered him, "I tell you the truth, today you will be with me in paradise."

Luke 23:43

Angels All Around

I wish our eyes could be opened to see the heavenly realms all around us. Elisha prayed that his servant's eyes might be opened to see the heavenly realities all around him. The Lord answered his request and the servant saw "... chariots of fire all around Elisha."

For Reflection

If your eyes were opened to see the heavenly realms and its hosts, who would you see and what would they be doing? Would you want to see the heavenly realms all the time? Why or why not? What difference can it make in your life, knowing that there are heavenly beings around us all the time?

_____

_____

_____

_____

_____

_____

_____

_____

_____

_____

_____

_____

And Elisha prayed, "O LORD, open his eyes so he may see." Then the LORD opened the servant's eyes, and he looked and saw the hills full of horses and chariots of fire all around Elisha.

2 Kings 6:17

Our Relationship With Angels

One of the best parts of heaven may be getting to know and fellow-shiping with angels. They love God and they enjoy us. If angels rejoiced so happily over our conversion (Luke 15:10), how much more will they rejoice over us when we arrive at the foot of God's throne.

For Reflection

If angels are sent to serve us, in what ways do they carry out their ministry? Have you sensed their ministry to you physically? Emotionally? Spiritually? What does the existence of angels say about God and his feelings toward us? How will you relate to angels once you are in heaven?

_____

_____

_____

_____

_____

_____

_____

_____

_____

_____

_____

_____

Are not all angels minister-
ing spirits sent to serve those
who will inherit salvation?
Hebrews 1:14

*M*y friend was steering me in my wheelchair through thick crowds and piles of suitcases in the baggage claim area of the Los Angeles airport. Angry passengers bemoaned lost luggage. A line of people jostled through a turnstile. Outside, taxis honked. Policemen hollered. It was a crazy ending to an even crazier day of bad weather and a late arrival. We found our luggage carousel and my friend parked my chair to go retrieve our things.

If you had seen me in that busy airport, you would have noticed a satisfied smile. With eyes of faith I looked beyond the sight of bumper-to-bumper traffic, the smell of sweat, cigarettes and exhaust fumes, the sounds of my harried co-travelers, and began humming quietly A.E. Brumley's song . . .

This world is not my home, I'm just a passing thru,
My treasures are laid up somewhere beyond the blue;
The angels beckon me from Heaven's open door,
And I can't feel at home in this world anymore.

I couldn't help seeing something past this world. How so? Because faith is double-sided. Through faith's eyes, heaven becomes a rock-solid home, and the concrete world in which we live becomes drained of substance and importance. *Because faith makes invisible things real, and visible things unreal, earthly dissatisfaction becomes the road to heavenly satisfaction.* One place, heaven, supplants the other, earth, as home.

Faith does another thing. The more homelike heaven becomes, the more you feel like an alien and stranger on earth. Take a minute to consider a time when you were actually homesick. Remember the aching. The sense of feeling like a stranger in your surroundings?

My most recent bout with homesickness was in Bucharest, Romania. It was the middle of the night and I knew I was an alien as soon as I wheeled into the musty hotel lobby. A single dangling light bulb cast long shadows over dusty sofas and lamps left over from the fifties. From somewhere behind the desk, a radio featured

Elvis Presley wailing "I Wanna Be Your Teddy Bear." There were bullet holes in the concrete wall. Moths and exhaust fumes filtered in through the open door and somebody was screaming at a neighbor down the street.

I was tired, hungry and dirty. There were no ramps for my wheelchair. I didn't fit in the bathroom. Everything about the place—the language, the culture, and especially the pillow on my mattress—made me long for California. It was awful. I know you've felt the same ... because home is where your heart is.

When you get homesick, your heart may tug for your own mattress and pillow, but this doesn't account for the gut-wrenching ache. What makes home is not a place, but who lives there. You feel at home when your heart is nestled near the one you love. When our heart melts into God's and when our mind is thinking on him, place and person no longer seem separated.

Use your eyes of faith here. God wants to get your mind racing and your heart beating with a present-tense excitement, a right-around-the-corner anticipation of heaven. Isn't that the way strangers on foreign soil are supposed to feel about their homeland?

I have a glorious homesickness for heaven, a penetrating and piercing ache. I'm a stranger in a strange land, a displaced person. I am looking forward to going home. Are you?

For Reflection

Think about a time when you felt homesick. What did it feel like? What did you do to make yourself feel better? Or could nothing make you feel better? If the word picture of homesickness describes your feelings about heaven, what can you do about it? Or will you always ache?

Forgetting what is behind and straining toward what is ahead, I press on toward the goal to win the prize for which God has called me heavenward in Christ Jesus.
Philippians 3:13b-14

Our Home in Heaven

Why Don't We Fit on Earth?

I wheeled through the Thousand Oaks Mall yesterday. I felt like a blessed stranger. Everyone seemed absorbed by the fashion show going on in the center courtyard, but I found myself thinking, *Does anyone else here realize that there's more to life than the new fall designs?*

For Reflection

Choose three things on earth you enjoy the most and then compare them with the preparations God is making for you. How do your "top three" stack up? God is sparing no expense to prepare a place for you.

Instead, they were longing for a better country—a heavenly one. Therefore God is not ashamed to be called their God, for he has prepared a city for them. Hebrews 11:16

Our Home in Heaven

Our True Identity

Our lost youth and lost identity are not to be recovered in the innocence of Eden. Only in heaven—the birthplace of our identity—will we find out who we truly are. Actually, we won't find it so much as receive it.

For Reflection

If it were your choice, what new name would you give yourself in heaven? Why that name? What advantage will our new selves have over the beings that would have been with Adam in the Garden of Eden before the Fall?

_____

_____

_____

_____

_____

_____

_____

_____

_____

_____

_____

_____

He who has an ear, let him hear what the Spirit says to the churches. To him who overcomes, I will give some of the hidden manna. I will also give him a white stone with a new name written on it, known only to him who receives it. Revelation 2:17

Our Home in Heaven

Why Don't We Fit?

As spiritual beings, you and I are not made for this world because the earth is temporal. There is something in us that is definitely *not* temporal. We squirm and groan against the confines of time. The clock, for us, is an adversary.

For Reflection

In what ways does time confine us and serve as our adversary? Are there also blessings to being confined by time? What blessings can you name for being a finite creature on earth?

There is a time for everything, and a season for every activity under heaven: a time to be born and a time to die, a time to plant and a time to uproot. Ecclesiastes 3:1-2

Our Home in Heaven

Face to Face

Here's a pop quiz for all you romantics: in whose face do we find ecstasy lasting? The points of eternity converge in the face of our Savior. Little wonder I not only want to paint in my mind the faces of friends I love, but also the face of Jesus.

For Reflection

How are you pursuing Christ? What can you do to nurture your "romance" with Jesus?

One thing I ask of the LORD, this is what I seek: that I may dwell in the house of the LORD all the days of my life, to gaze upon the beauty of the LORD and to seek him in his temple. Psalm 27:4

Our Home in Heaven

Our Place in Time

Jesus presented a kind of formula for our nature and destiny. The way our resurrected Lord was able to move through time and space is a prescription for our future heavenly experience. Jesus perfectly embodies physical things caught in time yet spiritual things that exist outside time.

For Reflection

Have you allowed your spirit a chance to grow since its birth, just as you have nurtured your physical body? How does the knowledge of a living, eternal, God-created spirit residing within you make you feel?

Flesh gives birth to flesh, but the Spirit gives birth to spirit. You should not be surprised at my saying, 'You must be born again.' The wind blows wherever it pleases. You hear its sound, but you cannot tell where it comes from or where it is going. So it is with everyone born of the Spirit. John 3:6-8

Our Home in Heaven

Too Heavenly Minded?

Sojourners who think the most of the next world are usually those who are doing the highest good in this one. C.S. Lewis expands on this, saying, "Aim at heaven and you get earth thrown in. Aim at earth and you get neither."

For Reflection

Colossians 3:2 calls on us to set our *minds* on Christ. How do we set our hearts on heaven, as Colossians 3:1 commands? How do we cultivate a useful affection for heaven that is good for us on earth?

_____

_____

_____

_____

_____

_____

_____

_____

_____

_____

_____

_____

_____

_____

Since, then, you have been raised with Christ, set your hearts on things above, where Christ is seated at the right hand of God. Colossians 3:1

Our Home in Heaven

Homesick for Heaven

It is to our benefit that we do not grow comfortable in a world destined for decay. We squirm and writhe, knowing we don't quite fit. But, oh, what a blessing those groans! What a sweetness to feel homesick for heaven.

For Reflection

What absorbs your attention on earth? Do you find it difficult to muster up longing for celestial mansions when earthly Grand Canyons are so beautiful? Pray for a divine dissatisfaction with everything pleasurable and wonderful on earth.

Meanwhile we groan,
longing to be clothed with
our heavenly dwelling.
2 Corinthians 5:2

Our Home in Heaven

Healing That Old Ache

When it comes to heaven, we want to be overpowered, enraptured and caught up in something grand and wonderful outside ourselves. We want to be swept and wrapped up in a joy that weaves itself through every nerve and fiber. Like Elijah's chariot, we want to be captured and carried away.

For Reflection

Think about what life would be like if you were totally possessed by heaven, caught up in it. What would your relationships with other people be like? How would you deal with trials and temptations? How would you make decisions?

*For where your treasure is,
there your heart will be also.*
Luke 12:34

Our Home in Heaven

In the Heart of God

Your heart's home is in the heart of God. He has placed within you a yearning for himself, a desire to know him and understand what he is like. Every soul feels the void and the emptiness until it connects with its Maker.

For Reflection

What is it about God that you seek? When you are finally held in His arms in heaven, what will you say to Him? How will you feel? Compose a petition to God, asking him to be your strength, your portion.

_____

_____

_____

_____

_____

_____

_____

_____

_____

_____

_____

_____

_____

_____

My flesh and my heart may fail, but God is the strength of my heart and my portion forever. Psalm 73:26

Our Home in Heaven

On Things Above

When you consider that the first and greatest commandment is to love the Lord with all your *heart and mind*, it follows that we should set our *entire being* (that's what it means when it says "heart and mind") on things above.

For Reflection

If your mind is set on heaven, is there any place that you could not live on earth? Is there any circumstance you could not endure? Is there any relationship to which you could not commit?

_____

_____

_____

_____

_____

_____

_____

_____

_____

_____

_____

_____

_____

Since, then, you have been raised with Christ, set your hearts on things above, where Christ is seated at the right hand of God. Colossians 3:1

Our Home in Heaven

Thinking God's Thoughts

It's no surprise God said to Isaiah, "My thoughts are not your thoughts." Somehow I don't think God stays up at night wondering why they don't standardize electric plugs worldwide. God's thoughts are higher than ours. My thoughts need to rise to the heavenlies where Christ is seated.

For Reflection

His thoughts and ways will always be higher than ours, but how can you begin to think and act like God today? What experience are you going through right now that needs some higher-order thinking and doing? Ask God to help you. After you've seen God working, come back to this point and record what happened.

_____

_____

_____

_____

_____

_____

_____

_____

_____

_____

_____

_____

"For my thoughts are not
your thoughts, neither are
your ways my ways,"
declares the LORD. "As the
heavens are higher than the
earth, so are my ways higher
than your ways and my
thoughts than your thoughts."
Isaiah 55:8-9

Our Home in Heaven

I Miss My Home

The nice things in this life are merely omens of even greater, more glorious things yet to come. God would not have us to mistake this world for a permanent dwelling. It's a good life, but I am looking forward to going home. I miss my home. I miss God.

For Reflection

What makes you long for the righteousness of heaven? Do you miss God *and* His righteousness? Pray that your longings for the righteousness of heaven will spur you to righteousness now.

But in keeping with his promise we are looking forward to a new heaven and a new earth, the home of righteousness. 2 Peter 3:13

In the early days of my paralysis when I first learned about heaven, I zeroed in on it because it was the place where I would receive new hands and feet. Heaven was the place I'd be freed from the pain. I felt as though the whole point of it was to get back all it owed me, all I had lost.

Time passed, and with it a little more spiritual maturity. It gradually dawned on me that the Day of Christ would be just that ... the Day of Christ, not the day of Joni. Glorified hands and feet, as well as reunions with loved ones, began to look more like fringe benefits.

Before we realize it, if we are blessed to be living at the time of his return, we shall find ourselves in the embrace of our Savior at the wedding supper of the Lamb. Heaven will have arrived. At first, the shock of joy may burn with the brilliant newness of being glorified, but in the next instant we will be at peace and feel at home, as though it were always this way, that we were born for such a place. At that moment, earth will seem like a half-forgotten dream, pleasant enough, but only a dream.

I glance down the table and there's my friend, Verna Estes, mother of seven swapping baby stories with Susanna Wesley, mother of seventeen. There's her pastor-husband, Steve, getting the low-down on Romans 6 from the apostle Paul. St. Augustine's giving a bear hug to that jungle missionary who labored long and hard, unknown and unnoticed. At the other end of the table, Fanny Crosby is doing harmony on one of her hymns with the widow who faithfully played the rickety piano at the nursing home every Sunday.

Then I'll look up and walking toward me will be Dad. And Mother. He'll give me his ol' thumbs-up and a wink, my mother will start giggling, and before you know it, we'll break up into uncontrollable laughter. We will laugh and cry with a kind of tears that never flowed on earth. And the party is just beginning.

We shall press in line with the great procession of the redeemed passing before the throne, an infinite cavalcade of nations and empires, age following age ... generations of the redeemed before the cross and after, all bearing their diadems before God Almighty. Together we will raise our voices, not in four-part harmony, but perhaps in twelve-part, with the twenty-four elders as "they lay their crowns before the throne" (Revelation 4:10).

The judgment seat of Christ may have been center stage where Jesus showered praise on the believer, but all of heaven will turn the spotlight on the Lord to give him back the glory. The universe will bow its knee and hail Jesus as King of Kings and Lord of Lords when he raises his sword in victory over death, the devil, disease and destruction.

But before he returns, while Christ is still in heaven, he is proclaiming through us the year of the Lord's favor, he is carrying out his agenda of compassion and forgiveness through you and me. He is still the tender, merciful shepherd, looking for more people to rescue, searching for lost men and women on whom he can gladly bestow salvation.

My responsibility as the betrothed is to be prepared ... and wait.

For Reflection

How are you actively proclaiming the "year of the Lord's favor" to those around you while you await Christ's return? List the names of those who as yet do not know Christ but with whom you want to reunite in heaven. Reflect on how you could boldly invite them to the banquet being prepared in heaven.

_____

_____

_____

_____

_____

_____   *After that, we who are still*
alive and are left will be
_____   *caught up together with them*
in the clouds to meet the
_____   *Lord in the air. And so we*
will be with the Lord forever.
_____   *1 Thessalonians 4:17*

Our Bridegroom and King

Be Prepared

God *will* find us and he will *not* always remain beyond our sight. Our bridegroom desires that I long and look for him "while we wait for the blessed hope." It's called being prepared. "It teaches us to say 'No' to ungodliness and worldly passions" (Titus 2:12).

For Reflection

Describe an experience when the thought of heaven or your reunion with Jesus kept you from yielding to temptation. Pray for many such experiences as a way to be prepared. Picture what it will be like in heaven, totally without sin. Record your thoughts and rejoice at the future freedom you will experience.

*Everyone who has this hope
in him purifies himself, just
as he is pure.* 1 John 3:3

Our Bridegroom and King

Waiting for the Groom

We may be separated from our Savior, but that's no reason to sit around, killing time until he comes. To wait is an occupation of the heart. To wait on the Lord is to love him with spirited affection. To wait on him is to fix your eyes on . . . Jesus.

For Reflection

Are you waiting on God for an answer to prayer? A concern that only he can satisfy? Have you ever simply waited for God and sought Jesus' presence? Fix your eyes on him today. Record your thoughts as you meditate on him.

_____

_____

_____

_____

_____

_____

_____

_____

_____

_____

_____

_____

_____

Wait for the LORD; be strong and take heart and wait for the LORD.
Psalm 27:14

Our Bridegroom and King

The Wedding Gift

It's a common practice for newlyweds to give gifts to each other. My gift to [Jesus] shall be whatever bits and pieces of earthly obedience I've done as evidence of my love. But what shall he give to us? He will give the joy of heaven.

For Reflection

What wedding gift are you bringing to the heavenly wedding supper of the Lamb? Have you experienced dynamic joy in your life here on earth? If so, how would you describe it? What were you doing or observing at the time? Remember that such joy is infinitely smaller than the joy that awaits you.

_____

_____

_____

_____

_____

_____

_____

_____

_____

_____

_____

_____

_____

And the ransomed of the LORD will return. They will enter Zion with singing; everlasting joy will crown their heads. Gladness and joy will overtake them, and sorrow and sighing will flee away. Isaiah 35:10

Our Bridegroom and King

Christ's Coronation Day

It will be Jesus' Day. We will delight in our reunion with loved ones, and yes, it will be exhilarating to reign over angels and rule the earth with new bodies too. But I have to keep remembering it will not be *our* celebration. It will be *his*.

For Reflection

If you were planning the marriage supper, what would you include in the program? Use your sanctified imagination to plan the ultimate wedding reception!

The twenty-four elders fall down before him who sits on the throne, and worship him who lives for ever and ever. They lay their crowns before the throne and say: "You are worthy, our Lord and God, to receive glory and honor and power." Revelation 4:10-11a

Our Bridegroom and King

Against All Odds

Any struggle between a hero and the bad guys is interesting, but when the hero is disadvantaged, a new element is introduced. Now the hero is in far more danger. If in his weakness he overcomes against all odds, he ends up twice as much the hero. The victory is awe-inspiring.

For Reflection

Why do we have such a hard time acting like Jesus is King? Is it because his battle tactics seem to throw us at the mercy of the devil? If victory is assured, what difference will it make in your life? What is there in your life that still needs to yield to Jesus the King?

And being found in appearance as a man, he humbled himself and became obedient to death—even death on a cross! Therefore God exalted him to the highest place and gave him the name that is above every name, that at the name of Jesus every knee should bow.
Philippians 2:8-10a

Our Bridegroom and King

The Terrible Day of the Lord

The same eyes that glowed with compassion will one day blaze with fire. Is this the Rose of Sharon, the Lily of the Valley? Lover and avenger? He is perfectly one and the same. And because he is perfect, his justice is pure.

For Reflection

Have you ever thought about the final judgment day? What will the people of the world have to fear from a judge whose eyes are like blazing fire and wearing a robe dipped in blood? What will you have to fear? What about God's justice causes you to rejoice?

_____

_____

_____

_____

_____

_____

_____

_____

_____

_____

_____

_____

_____

_____

_____

For with fire and with his sword the LORD will execute judgment upon all men, and many will be those slain by the LORD. Isaiah 66:16

Our Bridegroom and King

How Will We Feel?

Once in heaven, we will know in every fiber of our being, beyond a shadow of a doubt that whatever the judge declares about us is true. As he says we are, so are we. No more, no less. The self-evident truth about you or me will be clear to everyone.

For Reflection

If God were to judge your life apart from Christ, what would he decide regarding your destiny? Why? Is there anything about the fact that you will be self evident to everyone that causes you to cringe? Can you think of why this self-evident truth could be cause for hope and rejoicing?

It is a dreadful thing to fall into the hands of the living God. Hebrews 10:31

Our Bridegroom and King

Some Have Chosen Hell

The great judgment will be swift. C.S. Lewis says: "There are only two kinds of people in the end: those who say to God, 'Thy will be done,' and those to whom God says, in the end, '*Thy* will be done.' All that are in Hell, choose it."

For Reflection

If it were up to you, on whom would you direct God's wrath? Terrorists? Child pornographers? Drug dealers? Choose your top three. God will judge the wicked on that terrible day. Until then, pray that such people repent and turn to Christ .

_____

_____

_____

_____

_____

_____

_____

_____

_____

_____

_____

_____

_____

Out of his mouth comes a
sharp sword with which to
strike down the nations.
"He will rule them with an
iron scepter." He treads the
winepress of the fury of the
wrath of God Almighty.
Revelation 19:15

Our Bridegroom and King

Delaying God's Wrath

Jesus made it clear that his agenda was not to execute the wrath of God, but to bear in his own body that same wrath. He left off the most terrifying part of Isaiah 61:2 because he came to seek and save the lost . . . not to condemn or destroy.

For Reflection

Did you know that Jesus came to this earth to die on the cross and take God's white-hot anger against your sin? When the Lord returns he will crush the wicked. Will you end up getting trampled in the grapes of God's wrath?

"He has sent me to proclaim freedom for the prisoners and recovery of sight for the blind, to release the oppressed, to proclaim the year of the Lord's favor." Then he rolled up the scroll, gave it back to the attendant and sat down. Luke 4:18b-20a

Our Bridegroom and King

At Home With Our King

You and I were chosen to praise him. It's that simple. What a shame that on earth we made it so complicated.

For Reflection

You are the Father's gift to the Son. Are you pleased with what is being given to Jesus? Do you need to make any repairs on the gift of your life? Commit yourself to live the life you were called to live. And hurry, for the party is almost ready to begin.

_____

_____

_____

_____

_____

_____

_____

_____

_____

_____

_____

_____

_____

_____

_____

_____

Praise the LORD. Praise
God in his sanctuary;
praise him in his mighty
heavens. . . . Let everything
that has breath praise the
LORD. Praise the LORD.
Psalm 150:1,6

Our Bridegroom and King

Crown Him With Many Crowns

I wish we were standing together underneath a starry dome, feeling small and swallowed up, and tuning in to the faint and haunting melody of a hymn. We would lift our voices and sing along . . . "Crown Him with many crowns, The Lamb upon His throne . . . "

For Reflection

Is your blood pressure a notch higher as you contemplate our King on his throne? Are you awash in delight? Do you feel a deep reverence? Read the passage in Revelation 19 regarding the King and record your reactions.

_____

_____

_____

_____

_____

_____

_____

_____

_____

_____

_____

_____

_____

_____

His eyes are like blazing fire, and on his head are many crowns. He has a name written on him that no one knows but he himself. He is dressed in a robe dipped in blood, and his name is the Word of God. Revelation 19:12-13

The Journey Home

The faster time flies, the more precious my hours become. On some days, I feel as though I might be called Home any moment.

I had this "let's go home" feeling when I used to play in the woods beyond our back yard. As soon as I got home from elementary school, and while Mom was preparing dinner, I would put my things in my room and race out the back door to play tag with Kathy and a few neighborhood kids. We would call to each other and our shouts would echo through the tall oak trees. Everything echoed—the chatter of birds, the distant clatter of an old lawnmower, the slamming of screen doors. Our play was so much fun that an hour would go by and I'd hardly realize it. I barely noticed the rays of the sinking sun cutting long shadows through the trees. Kathy and I knew that soon Mom would call us home.

Funny, I rarely took it upon myself to go home unless called. I rather enjoyed hearing the sound of Daddy's or Mom's voice through cupped hands, shouting my name. No sooner did I hope they'd call when I would hear the familiar ding-ding-a-ling of the dinner bell by the back door.

"Supper's ready . . . time to come home!"

It's odd how I can still hear Mom's voice. The echo of that bell . . . the haunting sound through the woods . . . the joy about to break my heart open for the love of home . . . "Supper's ready . . . time to come home.". . .

Soon, much sooner than I realize, I will follow the sunset over the horizon . . . step into the other side of eternity . . . and partake of the wedding supper of the Lamb. And, oh, how good it will feel for us to rest, to be at Home.

I can remember how, after ten hours of riding my horse to check gates and fences, my weary mount would be wet with sweat, her head hanging low. I had to urge her to put one tired hoof in front of another. Then as soon as she caught a whiff of home or recognized the fences of her own pasture, her ears would prick up and

V

her pace would quicken. The nearer we came to the barn, the more eager her trot. After a quick unsaddling, she would joyfully roll in the dirt and take long deep drinks from the trough. How good it feels ... to be home, to be able to rest.

Maybe other writers of the Bible—some who had scars on their bodies from stonings, others whose joints were stiff from chains that chafed—had this sweet rest in mind, a rest that perked them up and quickened their pace. They wrote vigorous encouragements like, "Let us, therefore, make every effort to enter that rest," and "Seeing that the days are short, make every effort ... " and "Redeem the time for the days are evil."

Only the hope of heaven can truly move our passions off this world—which God knows could never fulfill us anyway—and place them where they will find their glorious fulfillment.

Enough has been wasted in your life. Don't waste any more of it. Don't worry about finding answers. Just use the time you've got. Make the most of every day ... as you follow the journey Home.

For Reflection

The existence of a rest in the future means that now is not the time to rest, but rather to work. From what will you rest when you get to heaven?

_____

_____

_____

_____

_____

_____   *There remains, then, a*
                                                   Sabbath-rest for the people
_____   *of God; for anyone who*
                                                   enters God's rest also rests
_____   *from his own work, just as*
                                                   God did from his. Let us,
_____   *therefore, make every effort to*
                                                   enter that rest, so that no one
_____   *will fall by following their*
                                                   example of disobedience.
_____   *Hebrews 4:9-11*

Getting Ready for Heaven

Eagles overcome the lower law of gravity by the higher law of flight. What is true for birds, is true for the soul. Souls that soar to heaven's heights on wings like eagles overcome the mud of earth that keeps us stuck to a temporal, limited perspective.

For Reflection

If you were an eagle, able to get a higher perspective on your current trial, what would you see and how would you respond? Why does a different perspective often change our attitude and our action about a situation? Pray that God's eagle eye be yours.

But those who hope in the LORD will renew their strength. They will soar on wings like eagles; they will run and not grow weary, they will walk and not be faint.
Isaiah 40:31

Suffering Prepares Us for Home

Just as Jesus exchanged the meaning of the cross from a symbol of torture to one of hope and salvation he gives me the grace to do the same with my chair. If a cross can become a blessing so can a wheelchair.

For Reflection

In what ways can your sufferings help you identify with Christ's suffering? What strengths have you found in your suffering?

_____

_____

_____

_____

_____

_____

_____

_____

_____

_____

_____

_____

_____

_____

That is why, for Christ's
sake, I delight in weaknesses,
in insults, in hardships,
in persecutions, in diffi-
culties. For when I am
weak, then I am strong.
2 Corinthians 12:10

The Journey Home

The End of Time View

Our life is but a blip on the eternal screen. Pain will be erased by a greater understanding; it will be eclipsed by a glorious result. Something so superb, so grandiose is going to happen at the world's finale, that it will suffice for every hurt and atone for every heartache.

For Reflection

Make a list of the things you are suffering right now. Next to each item write the words "It will pass and it will be worth it." Stand firm on God's promises and thank him that your life is a mist!

_____

_____

_____

_____

_____

_____

_____

_____

_____

_____

_____

_____

_____

_____

_____

_____

Why, you do not even know what will happen tomorrow. What is your life? You are a mist that appears for a little while and then vanishes.

James 4:14

The Journey Home

Suffering Points Us to Heaven

A broken heart leads to the true contentment of asking less of this life because more is coming in the next. The art of living with suffering is the art of readjusting your expectations in the here and now.

For Reflection

Begin asking less of this life. Try sharing your desires for heaven rather than your requests for today. Record your desires here and cultivate a regular habit of such prayer.

My flesh and my heart may fail, but God is the strength of my heart and my portion forever. Psalm 73:26

The Journey Home

Onward and Upward

God has placed suffering in your life to remind you that heaven is not only for the future; it is for now, for this present moment. Heaven is meant to bless your path and be a source of strength in your suffering today. Valiantly welcome it and greet it.

For Reflection

Pray for others who need the same comfort you've received in the midst of your suffering. Pray that they will get the same heavenly perspective.

For just as the sufferings of Christ flow over into our lives, so also through Christ our comfort overflows. If we are distressed, it is for your comfort and salvation; if we are comforted, it is for your comfort, which produces in you patient endurance of the same sufferings we suffer.
2 Corinthians 1:5-6

The Journey Home

Homeward Bound

God gives us timeless moments in the here and now, striking that resonant chord in our heart that echoes eternity. He woos us away from this world with that heavenly haunting ... those timeless moments when we send our hearts on ahead to heaven.

For Reflection

Choose one step of obedience you will take today and listen for that resonant chord in your heart when you take that step.

_____

_____

_____

_____

_____

_____

_____

_____

_____

_____

_____

_____

_____

_____

_____

_____

_____

_____

Be very careful, then,
how you live—not as unwise
but as wise, making the
most of every opportunity,
because the days are evil.
Ephesians 5:15-16

The Journey Home

Life Is Short

This is the kind of wisdom God wants you to apply to your twenty-four hour slices of time. This is the kind of wisdom that sends your heart on ahead to heaven. If we could only realize how short life is. Redeem the time. Make the most of your moments.

For Reflection

What is the purpose of your life? Are you using God's wisdom in your twenty-four hour slices of time? Are you investing for eternity? What do you need to do to make a good investment?

_____

_____

_____

_____

_____

_____

_____

_____

_____

_____

_____

_____

_____

_____

Teach us to number our days aright, that we may gain a heart of wisdom.
Psalm 90:12

The Journey Home

Twilight Years

Even the brightest day is sure to have its twilight. People who look up and see beyond the encroaching years enlarge their souls with . . . something eternal, not temporal. That's what children do who have no concept of time, and of such is the kingdom of heaven.

For Reflection

Do you sense the days getting shorter as you grow older? What qualities of a child do you need to cultivate in order to enlarge your soul?

_____

_____

_____

_____

_____

_____

_____

_____

_____

_____

_____

_____

_____

I tell you the truth, anyone who will not receive the kingdom of God like a little child will never enter it.

Luke 18:17

The Journey Home

Resurrection and Rest

I may only be cresting middle age, but like many of my friends who have toiled for years, I'm ready for a rest. No more wrestling against sin. No more prying the world's suction cups off my heart. No knock-down, drag-out fights with the devil.

For Reflection

Thank the Lord for His victory over *your* sin. Reflect on a body free from sin in heaven and a conscience free from sin too.

There remains, then, a
Sabbath-rest for the people
of God. Hebrews 4:9

The Journey Home

Seize the Day!

God gives us a twenty-four hour slice of time in which to make the most of every opportunity—opportunities that will have eternal repercussions. The way we spend ... the hours and moments counts. It counts far more than we realize.

For Reflection

Do you realize that there are only a few hours left in which to gain heavenly victories? How can you make the most of every opportunity the Lord sends your way? Can you sense the urgency of winning souls for Christ?

_____

_____

_____

_____

_____

_____

_____

_____

_____

_____

_____

_____

_____

_____

Therefore, as we have opportunity, let us do good to all people, especially to those who belong to the family of believers. Galatians 6:10

The Journey Home

Come Home!

When those tantalizing glimpses—those promises never quite ful-filled—find broader, more complete fulfillment in our maturing years, then we know we've found what we've longed for. The echoes are getting louder. They resonate. Someone is calling just a short distance away: "Come Home."

For Reflection

Can you sense Christ's call to "Come home?" Is his voice clearer? Has your heart learned to sense that resonant chord? Think about that last moment just before he calls you home. How will you answer Christ's call?

Instead, they were longing for a better country—a heavenly one. Therefore God is not ashamed to be called their God, for he has prepared a city for them. Hebrews 11:16